Morning, Noon, and Night

JEAN CRAIGHEAD GEORGE
Morning, Noon, and Night
PAINTINGS BY WENDELL MINOR

HARPERCOLLINS PUBLISHERS

Good morning, the dawn,
when the earth is turning from night to day
and waking begins.

The stork puts down his other foot.

The killdeer stretches her white-striped wings,

and the cardinal sings,

"Good morning, the sun. Cheer, Cheer."

Good morning, the morning,

when the earth has turned from dawn to light

and work begins.

The lark feeds her nestlings.

The eagle goes hunting.

Toads catch bugs. Flies bite their hardest,

and the bees buzz their message, "Work, Work."

Good noon, the noon,

when the earth has turned full face to the sun

and siesta is here.

The birds stop singing.

The antelopes doze.

The lizard hides. The snake lies still,

and the ground squirrels rest in their burrows.

Good afternoon, the afternoon,
when the earth is turning on toward the night
and work is done.

The magpie preens.

The marmot rests on his lookout rock.

The bison ambles to the water,
and the prairie dog romps with her young.

Good evening, the evening,

when the earth has turned from light to dusk

and vesper begins.

The deer walks in twilight.

The jackrabbit leaves her hideout to eat.

The elk grazes,

and the brook trout swallows

his last bug before dark.

Good night, the night,

when the earth has turned away from the sun

and the night folks are up.

The bat dips and flies.

The wolf frolics over the mountains.

The elephant seal dives deep for food,

and the owlet sings,

"Who, the night, Who, Who?"

And the earth keeps on turning,

on turning, on turning.

Good morning, the sun. "Cheer, cheer."

To Hunter, the newest sunshine in my life
—J.C.G.

To the memory of our cat, Mouse; we loved her morning, noon, and night
—W.M.

E N D N O T E S

Frontispiece:	mallard duck and ducklings in the Eastern Wetlands
pp. 4–5	dolphin on the Eastern Seaboard (Maine)
pp. 6–7	killdeer and cardinal in the Eastern Piedmont (North Carolina)
pp. 8–9	wren and oxen in the Heartland (Ohio)
pp. 10–11	honeybee and bald eagle over the Great Lakes
p. 13	bison and cowbird in the Great Plains (South Dakota)
pp. 14–15	pronghorn antelope and chuckwalla in the Mesaland (Arizona)
pp. 16–17	gosling and Canada goose in the Rocky Mountains' Front Range (Colorado)
pp. 18–19	magpie and whistling marmot in the Rocky Mountains (Wyoming)
pp. 20–21	bison and prairie dog and young in the Great Basin (Wyoming)
p. 23	bats in the Arizona–Sonora Desert (Arizona)
pp. 24–25	mule deer and elk in the High Sierras (California)
pp. 26–27	opossum and raccoon in the Redwood Forest (California)
pp. 28–29	owlet and elephant seal pup on the Pacific Coast (California)
pp. 30–31	cardinal and black-capped gull on the Eastern Seaboard (Maine island)

Morning, Noon, and Night • Text copyright © 1999 by Julie Productions, Inc. • Illustrations copyright © 1999 by Wendell Minor • Printed in the U.S.A. All rights reserved. • Library of Congress Cataloging-in-Publication Data George, Jean Craighead, date • Morning, noon, and night / by Jean Craighead George ; paintings by Wendell Minor p.   cm. • Summary: Each day as the sun makes its dawn-to-dusk journey from the Eastern seaboard to the Pacific coast, the animals perform their daily routines. • ISBN 0-06-023628-0. — ISBN 0-06-023629-9 (lib. bdg.) [1. Day—Fiction. 2. Animals—Fiction.] I. Minor, Wendell, ill. II. Title • PZ7.G2935Mo 1999 97-28796 CIP   AC • Typography by Wendell Minor and Al Cetta 1 2 3 4 5 6 7 8 9 10 ❖ First Edition